ENGLAND
of One Hundred Years Ago
PHOTOGRAPH
COLLECTION

FOREST OF DEAN

SELECTED BY HUMPHREY PHELPS

ALAN SUTTON

First published in the United Kingdom in 1992
by Alan Sutton Publishing Limited
Phoenix Mill, Stroud, Gloucestershire

First published in the United States of America
by Alan Sutton Publishing Incorporated
83 Washington Avenue, Dover, New Hampshire

British Library and Library of Congress
Cataloguing in Publication Data applied for

ISBN 0-7509-0303-1

Typesetting and origination by
Alan Sutton Publishing Limited
Graphics and Design Department.
Printed in Great Britain by
Bath Colour Books.

Some blemishes have been removed by extreme enlargement of the image to individual pixel level, with careful computer graphics surgery to mend scratches, foxing, or other damage to the photographic image.

WHITE HORSE
HOTEL
Commercial &
Posting House

Plate 22. A STRANGER IN TOWN
Mitcheldean, *c.* 1910

Plate 23. ALL ABOARD THE FERRY
The ferry at Newnham, *c.* 1908

Plate 24. THE SPEECH HOUSE
1900

Plate 25. MINERS' BREAK
The Robin Hood iron mine, Staunton, *c.* 1885

Plate 26. FOREST TUNNEL
Upper Soudley, *c.* 1914
(Dean Heritage Museum)

Plate 27. THE MILLPOND
The church at Westbury, *c.* 1912

Plate 28. LAST DAY OF THE TURNPIKE
Whitecliff, 1888